D1543124

◆—Westward Expansion◆—

AMERICA'S PUSH TO THE PACIFIC

THE GOLD RUSH

THERESA MORLOCK

Britannica
Educational Publishing

IN ASSOCIATION WITH

ROSEN
EDUCATIONAL SERVICES

Published in 2018 by Britannica Educational Publishing (a trademark of Ency-clopædia Britannica, Inc.) in association with The Rosen Publishing Group, Inc. 29 East 21st Street, New York, NY 10010

Copyright © 2018 The Rosen Publishing Group, Inc. and Encyclopædia Britannica, Inc. Britannica, Encyclopædia Britannica, and the Thistle logo are registered trademarks of Encyclopædia Britannica, Inc. All rights reserved.

Distributed exclusively by Rosen Publishing.
To see additional Britannica Educational Publishing titles, go to rosenpublishing.com.

First Edition

Britannica Educational Publishing
J.E. Luebering: Executive Director, Core Editorial
Andrea R. Field: Managing Editor, Compton's by Britannica

Rosen Publishing
Heather Moore Niver: Editor
Nelson Sá: Art Director
Tahara Anderson: Series Designer & Layout
Cindy Reiman: Photography Manager
Heather Moore Niver: Photo Researcher

Library of Congress Cataloging-in-Publication Data

Names: Morlock, Theresa, author.
Title: The gold rush / Theresa Morlock.
Description: New York, NY : Britannica Educational Publishing in Association with Rosen Educational Services, 2018 | Series: Westward expansion : America's push to the Pacific | Includes bibliographical references and index. | Audience: Grades 5–8.
Identifiers: LCCN 2017014834| ISBN 9781680487893 (library bound) | ISBN 9781680487886 (pbk.) | ISBN 9781538300503 (6 pack)
Subjects: LCSH: California—Gold discoveries--Juvenile literature. | California—History—1846-1850—Juvenile literature. | Frontier and pioneer life—California—Juvenile literature.
Classification: LCC F865 .M83 2018 | DDC 979.4/04—dc23
LC record available at https://lccn.loc.gov/2017014834

Manufactured in the United States of America

Photo credits: Cover, p. 32 Everett Historical/Shutterstock.com; p. 5 © iStockphoto.com/WildLivingArts; p. 9 Nagel Photography/Shutterstock.com; p. 10 Mary Evans Picture Library/Alamy Stock Photo; p. 12 Hulton Archive/Getty Images; p. 15 Ullstein Bild/Getty Images; pp. 17, 24, 34 MPI/Archive Photos/Getty Images; p. 18 Three Lions/Hulton Archive/Getty Images; p. 19 Rischgitz/Hulton Archive/Getty Images; pp. 20, 30, 38 Bettmann/Getty Images; p. 23 Bloomberg/Getty Images; p. 25 saraporn/Shutterstock.com; p. 27, cover and interior pages (banner) Library of Congress Prints and Photograph Division; p. 35 Universal Images Group/Getty Images; p. 40 Private Collection/The Stapleton Collection/Bridgeman Images; p. 41 North Wind Picture Archives/Alamy Stock Photo.

CONTENTS

INTRODUCTION

James W. Marshall was a thirty-seven-year-old carpenter building a sawmill along the American River in Coloma, California, when something shiny caught his eye on January 24, 1848. Could these glittering flakes actually be gold? Marshall gathered up the bright, yellow pieces and sped to the office of the mill's owner, John Sutter. Urging him to secrecy, Marshall showed Sutter his findings. Sutter tested the flakes and confirmed Marshall's suspicion: gold had been found in California. Within months, Marshall's discovery was made public, sparking a chain of events that transformed California and fueled the westward push of the United States.

In the years that followed Marshall's discovery, California's population exploded. Lured by the promise of riches and a new life, people from around the world flooded into California. Emigrants from Mexico, Chile, China, Australia, Germany, Ireland, and France came with the hope of striking it rich and returning home

Today, the Sutter's Mill site is part of Marshall Gold Discovery State Historic Park. The park includes a model of the original sawmill and many historic buildings.

with fortunes in their pockets. American gold seekers traveled west from the eastern states, migrating in such vast numbers that their passage stimulated advancements in transcontinental travel. People of diverse backgrounds and ethnicities traveled to California, selling their property and getting loans to afford the journey. Along the way, they risked danger and disease for a chance at gaining riches.

The influx of migrants had serious consequences for the many native peoples of California. The people whose ancestors had lived in California for thousands of years shared little of the prosperity brought to California by the Gold Rush. Many American Indians were involved in the Gold Rush from its earliest days but were mistreated by white settlers and reduced to positions as laborers with low wages. California's Indians were devastated by the many diseases that were brought by migrants during the late 1840s and throughout the 1850s. Before the Gold Rush, Indians made up most of California's population, numbering about 150,000. By 1870, however, only thirty thousand Indians remained. Many of them were moved to reservations, where living conditions were very poor. The settlements that arose in response to the Gold Rush and the environmental impact of gold mining made traditional Native American lifestyles impossible to maintain.

In 1849 alone, $10 million worth of gold was pulled from the ground, and over the next few years this number grew. In view of the huge amounts of money that could be made, and the rising lawlessness in mining settlements, politicians pushed to speed up the process of statehood. In 1850, California became the thirty-first state. The Gold Rush peaked in 1852, when $81 million worth of gold was extracted in California. Afterward, the number slowly declined. By the end of the 1850s, the Gold Rush was over, but its legacy would continue to influence California—and the nation—in the years to come.

CHAPTER ONE
THE PEOPLE OF CALIFORNIA

B y the time it came under the control of the United States in 1848, California had undergone many changes. For thousands of years before Europeans arrived in the Americas, California was home to hundreds of diverse American Indian groups. Spanish explorers reached California during the sixteenth century and formed trading relationships with the Indians. The Spanish claimed California but mostly ignored it until 1769, when they established a mission at San Diego with the aim of converting the Indians to Christianity. At the time, more than three hundred thousand Indians lived in California.

Over the next fifty years, the Spanish founded twenty more missions along the coast. Spanish families were given large grants of land and enjoyed political control of the region. This elite Spanish population living in California came to be known as the Californios.

California remained under Spanish control until 1821, when Mexico won independence from Spain. Under the Mexican government, the Californios retained much of their power and influence, and further land grants were given to Mexicans. In 1846, the United States declared war on Mexico. The Mexican-American War ended with the Treaty of Guadalupe-Hidalgo on February 2, 1848. The Mexican government ceded control of California to the United States just nine days after James Marshall had discovered gold in Coloma.

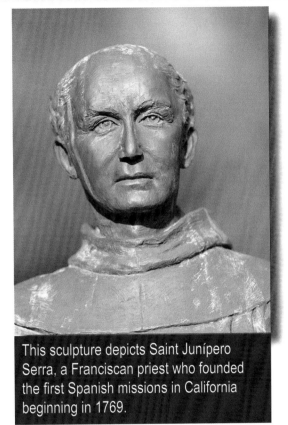

This sculpture depicts Saint Junípero Serra, a Franciscan priest who founded the first Spanish missions in California beginning in 1769.

WHO WERE THE FORTY-NINERS?

The first gold seekers to arrive in California came from the Sandwich Islands, which are now Hawaii, and from Oregon and Mexico. American settlers, African

THE BIG ANNOUNCEMENT

The news of Marshall's discovery was made public by a storekeeper by the name of Samuel Brannan in May 1848. Brannan visited the site and collected a bottle full of gold. He then traveled to San Francisco, where he flaunted the bottle and shouted "Gold! Gold! Gold from the American River!" People rushed from San Francisco to Coloma, where they bought many supplies from Brannan's store. Brannan's success during the Gold Rush made him California's first millionaire. He didn't mine for gold, but he made a fortune selling his goods to those who did.

SAMUEL BRANNAN, IN THE REGALIA OF PRESIDENT OF THE SOCIETY OF CALIFORNIA PIONEERS. (FROM A PAINTING IN THE SOCIETY ROOMS.)

Samuel Brannan.

Americans, Chinese immigrants, and many others soon followed. The tens of thousands who rushed to California in 1849 came to be called the Forty-niners. Altogether, they numbered more than eighty thousand.

By early 1849, an estimated six thousand Mexicans had come to California seeking gold. Although California had very recently been Mexico's property, Mexican miners were treated as outsiders and often suffered discrimination. The tension between Mexican and American miners was heightened by the fact that many Mexican miners were more experienced and successful than the Americans. In 1850, California passed a Foreign Miners Tax, which forced non-American miners to pay $20 a month to the state. This tax targeted Mexican miners to drive them out of California.

In 1852, the government imposed a new Foreign Miners Tax, this time aimed at removing the Chinese. Many people had left China because of the poor economic conditions that followed the first Opium War (1839–1842). The number of Chinese immigrants grew so much during the 1850s that they made up a fifth of the population in California's mining towns.

Some African American Forty-niners arrived in California as free people looking to make their own fortunes. Others were slaves brought by their owners. Free African American miners didn't have full rights as American citizens and were often mistreated by white

Taken in 1852, this photo depicts an African American miner at work in Auburn, California.

American miners. In 1850, California joined the Union as a free state, and many slaves gained their freedom. Nevertheless, slavery continued in some areas.

WOMEN IN THE GOLD RUSH

About 95 percent of the Forty-niners were men, typically white men from the eastern states. Married men usually left their families at home in the East, with the promise of returning with riches. In 1850, women made up less than 10 percent of California's population.

Despite their small numbers, women participated in the Gold Rush in many ways. Because many of the men who came west were accustomed to having their wives clean and cook for them, they paid women to perform these tasks. Some women made a living by running boarding-houses, where they housed and cooked for miners. With so few women in California, those who did live there found their skills and company to be in high demand.

Gold Rush women were divided socially and labeled as either "bad" or "good." During the mid-19th century, women were held to a different moral standard than men. Women who had nontraditional lifestyles or jobs were thought of as immoral and labeled "bad." One of the most famous "bad" women of the Gold Rush was Miss Ah Toy, a Chinese entertainer who lived in San Francisco.

CHAPTER TWO
THE JOURNEY

Whether coming from within the United States or from abroad, those who made the journey to California faced many risks. There were a number of routes to take to California. Chinese miners sailed across the Pacific Ocean, spending up to two months making the trip in small boats. The three main routes used by American gold seekers were the Oregon-California Trail, the Cape Horn route, and the Panama shortcut.

None of the routes to California were free from challenges or expense. Trips could cost $400 or more and lasted several months. Each of the routes attracted a different demographic of gold seekers. Those traveling with families usually made the journey overland as it was too expensive or too cramped to do so on a ship. People traveling overland could expect six months of hardship and many unpredictable accidents along the way. Thousands of people died before reaching their destination. The sea

This wood engraving from 1848 depicts travelers crossing through Panama during their long journey to San Francisco.

voyage around Cape Horn could last up to eight months. Although the route through Panama offered the shortest travel time (as little as a month), it required braving the many threats of the Panama jungle.

THE OREGON-CALIFORNIA TRAIL

The Oregon-California trail stretched more than 2,000 miles (3,200 km) from Missouri to

MANIFEST DESTINY

The westward expansion that took place during the nineteenth century was spurred by the idea of Manifest Destiny. Americans who believed in Manifest Destiny felt that it was their right and duty to spread their culture across the country. Manifest Destiny fueled the nation's growth because it instilled American settlers with the belief that God had chosen them to spread Protestant and democratic ideals to the vast West. Manifest Destiny had serious consequences for American Indians, who were forcibly removed from their lands to make way for American settlers.

Oregon and California. By wagon, the journey could take upwards of six months to complete. The main starting point of the trail was Independence, Missouri. Heavy wagons pulled by oxen, mules, or horses usually set off in wagon trains. These were groups of wagons that made the long, hard journey together. Banding together as a team offered advantages in terms of safety along the trail. A large wagon train could intimidate bandits or hostile American Indians who might consider attacking a lone wagon.

People in wagon trains also relied on each other for support when challenges arose. The varied terrain

Many travelers saw American Indians as a threat. This illustration, published in 1870, portrays a group of Indians who have attacked a wagon train and taken a captive.

across the country was a constant challenge for travelers. In wagon trains people could share supplies or lend a hand pushing the wagon or carrying loads across tough passes. In good conditions, a wagon could cover 12 to 20 miles (19 to 32 km) in a day. However, if the roads were muddy or there were rivers to cross, they were lucky to cover 5 miles (8 km). Other challenges of the journey included accidents and illness. Among the common trail diseases were cholera, smallpox, tuberculosis, diphtheria, typhoid fever, and scurvy.

TRANSCONTINENTAL TRAVEL

The huge demand for transportation to California gave rise to important developments in transcontinental travel. The influx of travelers through Panama inspired the creation of the Panama Railroad. Stretching from the Atlantic coast to the Pacific, it was the world's first transcontinental railroad. Construction began in 1850 and was completed five years later. In 1863, a few years after the end of the Gold Rush, workers began building the first transcontinental railroad in the United States. It was completed in 1869. When the Panama Canal was built in the early 20th century, it closely followed the route of the Panama Railroad. Though only about 51 miles (82 km) long, it had a huge impact on world trade.

The Panama Locomotive was one of the first trains to cross the Isthmus of Panama.

This illustration depicts travelers aboard a ship making the dangerous sea voyage around Cape Horn in 1849.

Despite the many dangers along the way, by the end of 1849 more than six thousand wagons carrying forty thousand people had traveled to California across the Oregon-California trail.

THE CAPE HORN ROUTE

The longest route to California was the sea voyage around Cape Horn, at the southern tip of

The Magnificent, Fast Sailing and favorite packet Ship,

JOSEPHINE,

BURTHEN 400 TONS, CAPT.

Built in the most superb manner of Live Oak, White Oak and Locust, for a New York and Liverpool Packet; thoroughly Copper-fastened and Coppered. She is a very fast sailer, having crossed the Atlantic from Liverpool to New-York in 14 days, the shortest passage ever made by a *Sailing Ship*. Has superior accommodations for Passengers, can take Gentlemen with their Ladies and families. Will probably reach SAN FRANCISCO **THIRTY DAYS** ahead of any Ship sailing at the same time. Will sail about the

10th November Next.

For Freight or Passage apply to the subscriber,

RODNEY FRENCH,

New Bedford, October 15th, **No. 103 North Water Street, Rodman's Wharf,**

Transportation companies created posters like this one to sell trips to gold country. The ship advertised in this announcement departed from New Bedford, Massachusetts.

South America. Gold seekers first boarded a ship in New York. The ship traveled south around Cape Horn and then north to California, where passengers would get off at San Francisco. The voyage took about six months. The Cape Horn route covered 18,000 nautical miles (33,000 km). During this lengthy trip passengers faced illness, hunger, and poor nutrition. Ships traveling the Cape Horn route were often very crowded, which caused sickness to spread quickly.

THE PANAMA SHORTCUT

A third route involved both sea and overland travel. The first step of the journey was to board a ship departing from the East coast of the United States and sailing to the Atlantic coast of Panama, in Central America. Then travelers crossed the Isthmus of Panama, the strip of land that connects North America and South America. They canoed up the Chagres River, in central Panama. Then they rode a mule through the jungle to reach Panama City on the Pacific coast. There they boarded a ship to San Francisco.

By taking the Panama shortcut, gold seekers could cut about 8,000 miles (13,000 km) and a few months off the Cape Horn route. Unfortunately, the advantages of the Panama shortcut came at a very steep price. Diseases such as yellow fever and malaria were a huge threat to travelers through Panama.

CHAPTER THREE
STAKING CLAIMS

The drive to get to California as quickly as possible was spurred by the fact that people were claiming mining territories on a first-come-first-served basis. Before it achieved statehood, California had no laws or government. In 1848, there was also no federal law to regulate mining. People came to California thinking that gold was free for the taking.

Rules about rights to property and how miners interacted were governed by a miners' code. This code served as a system by which property rights could be managed based on staking claims. Miners didn't own the property they claimed. However, the first person to get to a site, discover gold, and mine it was entitled to the gold he found. A person could maintain his claim to a site only if he notified other miners that it belonged to him. A miner's claim to a site lasted only

In 2014, a drought in Folsom, California, led to the discovery of artifacts from a Gold Rush settlement. The artifacts, pictured here, had previously been covered by Folsom Lake.

as long as the miner continued to work it. If a person left his mining site, he lost his claim to it. The site was considered free to be claimed by a new miner. Taking over a marked site that wasn't being worked was called "claim jumping."

Miners usually claimed a site and left within a short period of time. The Gold Rush was truly a race to find the site that would yield the most gold. Because no one knew exactly where the gold was or how much could be found, a miner would typically abandon an unproductive site quickly and then claim another.

LIFE IN MINING TOWNS

As mining camps began to form, each district established a set of rules. Without a government or other authority to enforce these rules, however, property claims were not very secure. The miners' code worked

This illustration, created by an artist named J Hesse, portrays emigrants arriving at the port of Sacramento in California during the Gold Rush.

only if people were willing to follow it. Many property rights were maintained only with the threat of violence, and disputes over claims were frequently settled with weapons rather than diplomacy. California's mining districts were thought of as lawless, violent, and immoral places.

Many men came to California with the attitude that the laws that governed their behavior at home didn't apply to them out west. Miners could spend twelve to sixteen hours a day, six days a week doing hard physical labor at their claim sites. They spent their Sundays off in mining towns, playing as hard as they worked. Alcohol was readily available in mining towns and so was opium. Without authorities to keep people in check, drunken bar brawls and petty fights could end in murder. Mining towns also presented men with plenty of opportunities to gamble.

Bodie State Historic Park is a preserved Gold Rush ghost town in eastern California. Mining towns became ghost towns when miners deserted them after the gold was gone.

Men in mining towns outnumbered women nine to one. The lack of women meant that mining town society was rougher and rowdier than in the East. Mining towns were, however, far more ethnically diverse than most towns in the United States during the mid-1800s. Chinese, Mexican, African American, and American Indian people interacted with each other and with white Americans to a degree that was unmatched in the East. Unfortunately, prejudice and racism were common, and some of the violence that occurred in mining towns was racially driven.

SLAVERY

In 1848, about half of the gold diggers in California were American Indians. These diggers were expected to perform the hardest labor for the lowest price. In 1850, the California legislature passed the Act for the Government and Protection of Indians. The act created a list of American Indian crimes and punishments and denied Indians the right to testify in court. Under the terms of the act, American Indians could be seized and forced to do involuntary labor. In effect, the act allowed white people to enslave Indians. An amendment to the act in 1860 allowed whites to take orphaned Indian children as slaves and force them to serve until they reached thirty-five to forty years of age.

RACIAL VIOLENCE

The American Indians of California suffered the worst of the racial violence that occurred during the Gold Rush. When the Forty-niners flooded California, they overran American Indian lands. Most white Americans felt that the Indians stood in the way of progress. Indian communities were attacked by groups of miners who wanted to stake claims on their land. In some instances, entire villages were murdered. Many Indians were forced to march to reservations, where conditions were dismal and many people starved.

Tragically, the abuse of American Indians was widely accepted and even encouraged. In certain California districts, miners were paid for Indians' body parts and scalps. The popular attitude was that Indian lives were worthless. Gold Rush

In a photograph from about 1924, a Pomo Indian uses a tool called a seed beater to knock seeds off plants and into a basket. Following the influx of settlers sparked by the Gold Rush, the Indians of California found it increasingly difficult to maintain their traditional lifestyles.

miners didn't just deny American Indians their right to land, they denied their right to life. The belief in white superiority and Manifest Destiny was supported by the United States government's brutal treatment of American Indians across the country.

The miners also carried diseases to which the American Indians had no immunity. Smallpox, measles, and cholera spread quickly, killing thousands of Indians. It has been estimated that disease was responsible for 60 percent of the American Indian population losses during the mid-1800s.

CHAPTER FOUR
MINING METHODS

Immigrants and American settlers were lured west by newspaper advertisements claiming that California was a land of "inexhaustible gold mines" where any man could strike it rich. These ads often made light of the challenges that miners would face when they arrived. Few of the people who came to California were prepared for the grueling realities of gold mining. Some men spent hours standing knee-deep in frigid creeks as they hopefully panned for gold. Others faced extreme risks digging and blasting for gold. Most of the Forty-niners had no mining experience or skills and had to learn through trial and error. Even with very hard work, few miners actually achieved the success they dreamed of.

During the 1850s, the amount of available gold began to decline. New mining techniques evolved

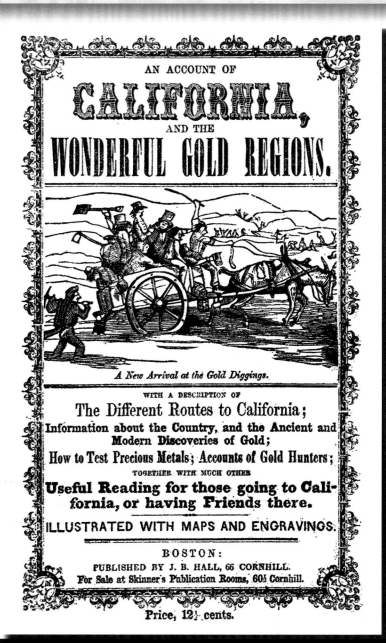

The book pictured here was published in 1849. It offered readers descriptions of the routes to California as well as helpful information about mining techniques.

to reach the gold that remained further below the surface. As mining technology advanced, the character of gold mining in California changed. Mining by individuals who worked their own claims was replaced by large-scale industrial mining. Rather than seeking their own fortunes, miners were hired to work in mines owned by corporations. The new mining techniques employed by these companies had a devastating impact on California's environment and landscape.

BONANZA!

Gold isn't usually found in pure, collectible nuggets, but in mineral ores. An ore is a naturally occurring mineral or combination of minerals that contains a valuable material such as a precious metal. In gold mining, the word bonanza is used to describe a large, valuable mineral deposit. Ground that contains large quantities of gold-bearing ore is called "pay dirt." At the beginning of the Gold Rush, bonanzas and pay dirt were readily available and miners could find gold using tools they could operate on their own. After the valuable ore was mined from the surface, however, miners had to work together to extract deeper ores. This led to the shift from individual mining to industrial mining.

EARLY TECHNIQUES

Panning was the simplest way of collecting gold. It involved scooping soil or gravel from the bottom of a stream into a shallow pan. The person would then

This illustration from 1849 depicts the panning method used by many gold miners.

swirl the water in the pan so that the heavier pieces of gold would sink to the bottom while the lighter material—dirt and gravel—would come to the surface. The miner tilted the pan to allow the dirt and gravel to wash away, leaving only the gold behind. Panning was the slowest and least effective method of collecting gold. Miners could typically get through fifty pans in a day and collect only a small amount of gold.

The rocker, or cradle, was a machine developed to speed up this process. A rocker was a long wooden box mounted on two curved pieces of wood similar to the curved runners of a rocking chair or baby's cradle. The box was set at a downward angle. The miner shoveled dirt into the box and then poured water over it. The material was sifted by rocking the box from side to side. As the material was washed along, barriers called riffles captured pieces of gold, which were then collected by hand.

Later devices used the same concept as the rocker but improved on it. The long tom was bigger than the rocker and therefore could handle more material. It also contained a sheet of metal with holes in it to aid the sifting process. The long tom evolved into the sluice box, an even longer version of the same device. A sluice box was placed in a running stream, making it more efficient than devices in which water had to be supplied by hand.

WASHING WITH THE LONG TOM, NEAR MURPHY'S.

This illustration from 1860 portrays miners working a long tom. This device for separating gold from dirt and rocks was an improvement on the rocker because it could handle more material.

HYDRAULIC MINING

Hydraulic mining used jets of water to break apart hard rock to reach the gold ore inside. The water was piped through a hose and blasted out through a nozzle. The powerful stream was shot at a hillside, breaking the hard rock into pieces. The water and blasted rock flowed through sluice boxes to collect the gold. The unwanted material was washed or dumped into nearby streams and rivers.

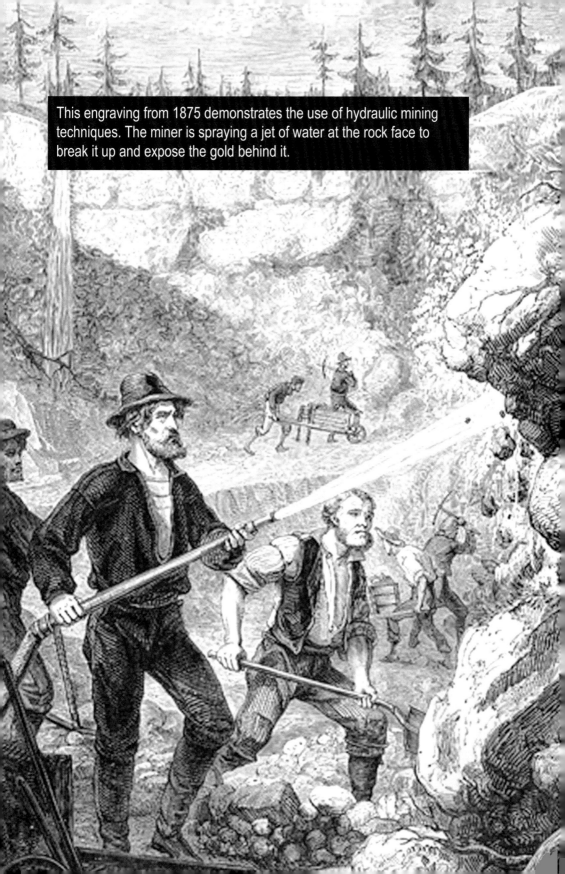

This engraving from 1875 demonstrates the use of hydraulic mining techniques. The miner is spraying a jet of water at the rock face to break it up and expose the gold behind it.

Hydraulic mining permanently changed the landscape of northern California. The debris left behind from blasting the Sierra Nevada mountains clogged rivers and streams flowing toward San Francisco Bay. Along with blocking navigation on these rivers, the debris caused them to frequently overflow their banks. Flooding spread silt and sand over farmland in the Sacramento Valley, which was disastrous for many farmers. Mining debris also killed wildlife in the rivers and upset the natural balance of ecosystems.

Hydraulic mining was very profitable, and for some time the environmental damage it caused was overlooked because of the gold that it yielded. In time, however, the mounting issues it created led to an outcry against its use. Hydraulic mining eventually shut down as it became too problematic and too expensive.

CHAPTER FIVE

THE GOLD RUSH LEGACY

The Gold Rush transformed the people, culture, economy, and landscape of California in profound ways. California was rapidly converted from a rural, inaccessible region to a populous territory filled with booming towns and cities. The Gold Rush spurred advancements in transportation, which made transcontinental travel in the United States more available than ever before. Technological advancements caused mining to shift from being an endeavor of the individual to a corporate industry. The influx of immigrants to California made it a place of multiculturalism and ethnic diversity.

In the years that followed the Gold Rush, the period and the changes it brought about were somewhat romanticized. This chapter of American history was told as the story of single, white, American men risking everything to go west and claim their fortunes. The American miners were portrayed as daring, hardworking, and admirable symbols of Manifest Destiny. However, white American miners represented only one version of the Gold Rush story.

ALTERNATIVE PERSPECTIVES

For many white Americans, the Gold Rush represented the fulfillment of Manifest Destiny. The West was "civilized" according to common ideals of the time: the American Indians were almost entirely removed, the environment was dominated and its resources plundered, and the American way of life was spread from coast to coast.

THE MINER.

This woodcut portrays the popular image of the Forty-niner: a strapping, independent white man working his claim.

To understand the Gold Rush more fully, however, it's necessary to acknowledge alternative perspectives on the era. The discovery of gold in California fueled the region's growth and economy. However, destructive mining techniques permanently damaged the environment. The Gold Rush drew enormous numbers of immigrants from around the world, making California one of the most culturally diverse places in the United States. However, competition between ethnic groups gave rise to violence and ethnic oppression.

Government-sanctioned discrimination against Mexican and Chinese miners and the exploitation of American Indians are clear evidence that the period was not a golden age for everyone involved. Discriminatory laws against immigrant miners and the taxes that were demanded of them illustrate how minority groups were denied social, political, and economic equality. For California's Indians in particular, the Gold Rush was a tragedy. In the stampede to stake claims, Indians were systematically murdered and driven off their lands. Diseases wreaked havoc on their populations, and laws allowed white Americans to enslave them. The romanticized picture of the era has to be balanced with the viewpoints of the Indians and other groups who suffered because of the lust for gold.

THE SLAVERY QUESTION AND THE CIVIL WAR

The Gold Rush, and the growth it brought, thrust California into the heated national debate over slavery. Although at the start of the 1850s the African American

MINING LIFE IN CALIFORNIA.

Made in 1857, this engraving illustrates life in a Chinese mining camp during the Gold Rush. Chinese and other minority miners experienced discriminatory laws and hostility from white miners.

population in California numbered fewer than one thousand, California's position regarding slavery would weigh heavily in the precarious relationship between the Northern and Southern states.

On September 9, 1850, California joined the United States as the thirty-first state. The process of granting statehood to California had been expedited in light of the population explosion brought on by the Gold Rush. Another factor was the lawlessness that was growing there in the absence of an official state government.

Although there was much momentum to bring California into the Union, there was also much controversy over its status in regard to slavery. At the time, the nation had equal numbers of free states, where slavery was illegal, and slave states, where slavery was allowed. California petitioned Congress to enter the Union as a free state, which would upset the balance of free and slave states. The dispute threatened to break up the Union.

After months of debate, Congress finally passed the Compromise of 1850. The South agreed to allow

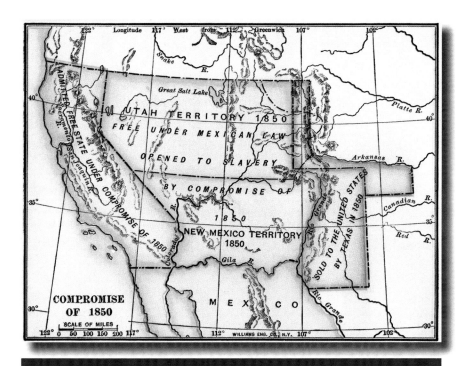

This map shows the status of slavery in the southwestern United States following the Compromise of 1850.

California to enter the Union as a free state and accepted the prohibition of the slave trade in the District of Columbia. In return, the North allowed New Mexico and Utah to organize as territories with no mention of slavery and gave the South a stronger fugitive slave law.

The Compromise of 1850 postponed but could not prevent war between the North and the South. After the American Civil War began in 1861, California's gold proved to be an important resource for the Union. In that time of crisis, gold shipments from the Sierra Nevada funded the US government and its war effort. This contribution to the Union victory was yet another legacy of the Gold Rush.

GLOSSARY

cede To yield or grant, typically by official agreement.

demographic The structure of a population.

diplomacy The practice of handling or negotiating a situation without hostility.

discrimination Treating a person badly or unfairly just because he or she is different.

elite Belonging to a small group of people within a larger group who have more power, privileges, or wealth than the rest of the group.

emigrant A person who has left a country to live somewhere else.

endeavor An enterprise or attempt to do something.

expedite To accelerate or speed up a process.

extract To take one item out of another.

flaunt To display something in a way that catches people's attention.

grueling Requiring extreme effort; exhausting.

hardship Deprivation and suffering.

influx A coming in.

instill To impart a feeling.

isthmus A narrow strip of land connecting two larger bodies of land.

precarious Dependent on uncertain circumstances.

reservation An area of land set aside by the government for American Indians to live on.

retain To keep in possession or use.

sanction To provide authoritative permission or approval.

transcontinental Extending across a continent.

FOR FURTHER READING

Benoit, Peter. *The California Gold Rush.* New York, NY: Children's Press, 2013.

Collins, Terry. *Stake a Claim!: Nickolas Flux and the California Gold Rush.* Mankato, MN: Capstone Press, 2014.

Hall, Brianna. *Strike It Rich! The Story of the California Gold Rush.* Mankato, MN: Capstone Press, 2015.

Maxwell-Long, Thomas. *Daily Life During the California Gold Rush.* Santa Barbara, CA: Greenwood Publishing Group, Inc., 2014.

Micklos, John, Jr. *A Primary Source History of the Gold Rush.* Mankato, MN: Capstone Press, 2016.

Onsgard, Bethany. *Life During the California Gold Rush.* Minneapolis, MN: Core Library, 2015.

Raum, Elizabeth. *The California Gold Rush: An Interactive History Adventure.* Mankato, MN: Capstone Press, 2016.

WEBSITES

Because of the changing nature of internet links, Rosen Publishing has developed an online list of websites related to the subject of this book. This site is updated regularly. Please use this link to access this list:

http://www.rosenlinks.com/WEST/Gold

INDEX